WHEN YOU'VE HIT ROCK BOTTOM

SMILE

YOU'RE NOT FALLING ANYMORE

Rodney Bonnet

©2018 RODNEY BONNET. All Rights Reserved.

ISBN-13: 78-1986740661

ISBN-10:1986740668

Published by
Dr. Shoneika Moore
P.O. Box 2592
Wilmington DE 19805

Cover design by: Dr. Shoneika Moore
Edited by: Critique Editing Services, LLC

Dedication

I dedicate this book to every single person who has experienced the numbing sensation of being at rock bottom. You've been assaulted by the challenges of failures, shortcomings, embarrassments, and disappointments, only to be left to endure life with the virus of mediocrity. May this book serve as the roadmap you need to relaunch the new and improved you.

Enjoy and appreciate the ride!

Acknowledgements

The manifestation of this book is a result of the blessed relationships I've had the privilege and opportunity to participate in.

To my parents: **Octanor and Paulette Bonnet**. For being the support I needed when I was at my lowest points in life. For bending my ears even when I didn't want to listen, you continue to plant the seeds that have made me the man I am today. For praying for me, when I couldn't muster the courage to pray for myself. Most importantly, for continually reaching out your hand to help me up from my many rock bottom places. I thank you, appreciate you and will always be grateful for you.

To my siblings **Ferentz, Kurtis, Merline and Orlane**, despite my faults, you have always had my back. You may have had an opinion, but you were always there.

To my spiritual parents **Bishop Matthew C. Haskell and Pastor Monica Haskell**, for taking the time to be the example I needed to become better, for raising the standards and making me grow as I reach to achieve them, for pulling my ear when my actions didn't line up with my confession, and most importantly, for loving the way you do and making it impossible not to ignore the prevailing call upon my life.

To **Jehan Janell Mahon**, one of the best friends I could ever have, for being the verbal acrobat that you are and forcing me to expand my thinking and be greater, for the advice you gave in a way only you could give it, for not allowing me to accept average by any means, and for showing that true friendship is real...it may have some bad days, even awkward ones, but in the end it's the reality of one's genuineness that matters.

To **Shawn Flemming**, for standing in the gap and allowing God to use you to minister to me, for being a keep-it-real type of brother who gave me the unfiltered truth even when I didn't want to hear it, most importantly, for being the love of God I needed when you saw me that day and said as you always do, "Ya good?"

Lastly, to a young lady who has become my present and will be my future, **Dr. Shoneika L. Moore**, for being the support I needed to make this project a reality, for challenging me when it all seemed overwhelming, for taking on roles to alleviate some of my burdens, and for loving me the way you do. It is your smile that brightens up my day, but your love that keeps me going.

Table of Contents

Foreword

Oh what a joy it is to see my spiritual son and mentee Rodney Bonnet move past life's obstacles, "Rock Bottom," and skyrocket into destiny. Utilizing emerging insights, and practical principles, Rodney shows you how to win with the hand you've been dealt.

I encourage you to read this book and use it as a rubric to catapult you towards your dream life.

Pastor Monica Haskell
CEO, PM Global

Introduction

Have you ever been in a place where absolutely nothing makes sense? You look around and see that the bottom has fallen out of every area of your life. You're standing in a room full of people; however, you feel so alone. You've fallen from a place that you thought was established, and it all comes crashing down like a plane out of gas falling at rapid uncontrollable speeds, crashing to the ground leaving no survivors.

At one point in time, we all have experienced that very scenario, where the life has been sucked out of us. Our bodies are numb from being poked by the anesthesia needles of hurt, shame, betrayal, abandonment, exclusion, and emotional castration. We have become well acquainted with that hard, cold lonely place known as Rock Bottom. I have been in this place many times in my life. I've been seated in a corner in the fetal position, hurt, beaten, and abused by life wondering, what do I do now? How do I bounce back from this situation? God, why me? I have felt as if I was worth nothing more than just to survive, barely existing. When I stepped out of the four corners of my life, I put on a smile and no one really knew what I was going through.

I dressed up very well, to the point where those around me thought I was on top of the world. Little did they know I was plotting ways to no longer exist, the pain was so grueling. I put on a disguise just to survive because that was all I knew how to do. I did this for a while until one Sunday one of my covenant brothers Shawn asked me, "Are you okay?" As was customary I said I was fine and played it off as if my pain were nothing. Little did I know that was the day my life would change, and never be the same again. Shawn persisted. He wouldn't let go of my hand until I was looking him in the eyes, and he asked again, "Really, are you okay?" For the first time I broke, and my eyes started to fill with tears and I finally said, "No."

My liberation came from finally seeing that I was not okay. My life was falling apart before my eyes, and I had no idea what I needed to do to fix it. It wasn't until I was honest with myself that I began the journey back to me. This liberation put me in a place where I was the most uncomfortable, causing me to doubt myself at times. I wondered if life was even worth living. Until I realized that I had tried everything else up to that point, so why not take a chance on me for once.

It wasn't until I was disgusted with what I saw in my life, in my bank account, and in the mirror, that I drew a line in the sand and restarted the journey back to me. In this book I will share with you seven principles that helped me change and refocus my life.

Chapter 1: Realize Where You Really Are

One of the most interesting things I have observed is how people use a GPS system. They input a destination and hit go. Automatically the GPS starts calculating routes and an estimated time of arrival, for each route. The interesting thing is that the GPS always gives you the option to enter your starting point as your "current location," or one that you would like to use as your starting point. Almost instinctually, we all use the current location. I have come to the conclusion that this is for a couple of reasons: it's easier, we're lazy, or more importantly, we just don't have a clue. I have come to the conclusion that we just don't know there are other options.

Sadly enough, we have been programmed to depend on others to do the thinking for us. Our "microwave society" thinking has handicapped us and made us dependent on outside influences to manage our lives.

We want everything in a hurry; we have lost the virtue of patience.

Everything we do is based on a reaction, and impulse, which causes

a ripple effect in all that is connected to us. The current condition of

where we are right now is based on the impulse decisions we made

five years ago. So, if we are looking to make changes in our future,

we need to start making better decisions now. In order for us to

realize where we are three things have to happen: admit that we are

lost, ask for guidance, and adjust.

Admit

The first of these three in most cases is the hardest, to admit

that you don't have a clue where you are. From birth we have prided

ourselves in knowing. We have created competitions such as

spelling bees, just to see who "knows" how to spell the most words.

That same spelling bee has morphed into the *Wheel of Fortune*,

where we compete on spelling various phrases to win cash. In no

way am I saying that healthy competition is bad. What I am referring

to is the ridiculing and belittling of those who *don't* know.

Challenges exist on all levels. However, for some who have overcome, they so easily forget how difficult it was for them to make it past that one hurdle. For this particular reason, many are afraid to say that they "don't know." It is these types of thoughts which create decisions, which create habits, which create a series of routines, which ultimately result in a lifestyle. Until we get to the root—the crippling thoughts—and admit that we are lost, no true change will happen. As humans we change our minds based on one of two influences, one being pleasure, the other being pain.

Ask

After we have taken the time to admit we don't know where we are, we have to be willing to ask for help. One of the challenges I had was I didn't want people to know I needed help. Most of what I was taught was to "suck it up and keep grinding." That is one of the hardest things to do when your spirit is broken. Out of habit I began to displace all my emotions and put on the mask that displayed I was actually okay. When I stepped outside of the four corners of my house, I put on a smile and acted like all was well. I was in a new place where most of the people who I came in contact with were not part of my past, so they only knew what I showed them.

I was living with a wound that I kept wrapping bandages around, never really treating the issue. I spent so much time hiding the infected spirit that it started to slowly decay. Everything connected to me was experiencing the effects of my decision to say nothing about my pain. I began to dull the pain by making myself so busy, I didn't have time to deal with the pain. It wasn't until the morning I looked in the mirror and didn't recognize my own reflection. I began believing the lies I told people to the point that it became the only reality I knew. I became numb with the Novocain of my lies. It wasn't until that morning when I looked in the mirror and didn't recognize the person staring back at me. The Novocain was wearing off and the pain was raging back with a vengeance. This was the morning when I put on the mask one more time, but I carried a burden that was heavy on me. It was the morning when Shawn asked me if I was okay and I was honest. It was the morning I finally asked for help. I put my pride in my pocket and reached out for the help I needed to survive.

The word "ask" is a verb, an action word, which can be defined as "to try to get by using words, request." This was the area of my life where I was the most uncomfortable, the pain was unbearable. Prior to that point I created an environment around me with my lies that became my new normal. However, it wasn't until reality hit that my pain required me to ask for help. I had to become uncomfortable and reach out for help. I was put in a position where I had to place my pride to the side if I wanted to live. No more could I continue to tell the lies, saying that everything was okay. I was tired of living a life that amounted to nothing at all; I was tired of just existing.

I wasn't just focused on asking for help, I was focused on learning from someone who had the life that I wanted. Too often we spend time asking for advice from people who are in our same situation, or worse. They are only able to give us knowledge of where they are, and in most cases it's not where we want to be. I had to learn that if I wanted better, I had to be around better—my life depended on it. I had spent too much time negotiating the outcome of my life using the wrong information. I had been operating my life with outdated and irrelevant information.

I just existed in a circle that was not challenging me; I was staying in the same position and going nowhere. I was in essence chasing a parked car. The only way for my life to change was for me to reach out to those who were moving. I had to find a coach, a mentor, an advisor who would not only understand my current situation, but also give me real, sound advice or instruction on how to change it.

Adjust

After we have taken the time to admit we are lost and need help, and have asked for help, we have to be willing to adjust to the instructions we have been given. When we look at the definition of the word adjust we see "to change (something) so that it fits, corresponds, or to conform, adapt, accommodate." The interesting part of the definition is the word "change." This one word has caused people to be uncomfortable because it requires an intentional shift away from our comfort zone. While the newfound instruction is amazing, it will only be theory until it's taken in and applied. We have to be willing to make the calculated decision to adjust and trust the process. Too many times we put so much stock in our comfort zone that we violently oppose change.

Our philosophies create a series of words, which create a series of actions, which create habits, which eventually create a lifestyle. This is the lifestyle that becomes our comfort zone.

It wasn't until I came face to face with my broken reality—the comfort zone that was actually killing me—did I decide to adjust and change. I received the advice and instruction and started to apply them at a not-knowing level, knowing that something had to really change. The more I adjusted, the more the change started to happen. I started seeing my life move in a positive direction and wanted more. So I continued to make adjustments and started to watch one breakthrough after another occur. I realized that what Jim Rohn said was true, "In order for your life to change, you have to change." Nothing was going to happen until I changed my thinking. When we look at movies like *Coach Carter*, and *Remember the Titans*, we can see a mental shift had to happen before any winning could be evident. Both Samuel L. Jackson (Coach Carter) and Denzel Washington (Coach Boone) had to alter the minds of the ones they were leading. But more importantly they had to believe in the change they were responsible for.

In both of these movies, the players were reluctant to change at first; however, they eventually realized the only way they would be able to win would be to adjust to the new way of thinking. Once they did that, once they were willing to make the conscious decision to adjust, life as they knew it transformed for the better.

Let's recap:

1. Admit and accept that you are lost and need direction to get to your destiny. Be willing to face the reality that the life you are living will not produce valuable fruit.

2. Ask for help. Look for a mentor, coach or advisor who will stretch you past your potential.

3. Adjust to the new normal. Stir up the courage necessary to change your philosophies, which will change your words, which will change your actions, which will change your habits, which will eventually change your lifestyle.

Chapter 2: Resolve to Change Your Outcome

"Determination gives you the resolve to keep going in spite of the roadblocks that lay before you."
– Denis Waitley

After you have taken the time to realize where you are, you have to resolve that the outcome of your life has to become better. Keeping things as they are will not only give you the same result, but also make you the target for average and mediocrity. Albert Einstein said, "Insanity: doing the same thing over and over and expecting a different result." Too many times we continue our mundane routines and wonder why nothing is changing. We operate using a passive playbook and get upset when we haven't moved one yard. We live life in expectation of a momentum shift; however, we never create or change our position to cause the shift. If we are looking for the current condition of our lives to change, we have to make a deliberate conscious decision to stop and change. We have to slam on the brake to stop the momentum of the wrong philosophies, words, actions and behaviours to change the direction. This is what is called resolve.

The definition of resolve is "to come to a definite or earnest decision about; determine (to do something)."

In this step you are going to choose to stop everything, nothing moves without being re-evaluated. See how the decisions you have made up to this point have gotten you to allow the vehicle of your life to make it to the top of a steep hill, then start to roll down that steep hill, picking up momentum as it descends. At the top of the hill you started not to care, and dosed off, not realizing you were putting yourself in danger. As this vehicle of your life is losing control, two things can happen: you can allow it to roll out of control and fall to your death or resolve to stop the vehicle and regain control. If you choose to do nothing, not only will you get hurt, but you will also put the lives of others in danger of being affected by your decision. Making the decision to slam on the brakes and stop the car, gives you the opportunity to change the outcome. In order to take a position of resolve, three things have to happen: Stop the current momentum, shift your thinking, and Show up for your rescue.

Stop

The momentum of the vehicle of your life has accelerated to the point where you only have two options, decide to live or die.

To some that may seem harsh; however, it is real. This is the life we live, absent-minded survival, just merely existing. We allow any and everything in our environment to decide for us and direct our vehicle, but they are not driving. We live based on their opinions and suggestions, not realizing that by doing so we are buying into their lifestyle. They don't have what we want, aren't headed in our direction, they don't have any of our beliefs. It is their influence that creates obstacles that we overlook. We subconsciously buy into their twisted thinking and create actions and habits that put us into a tornado we can't control. The only way we can change this negative momentum is to stop the car and slam on the brakes. Nothing will happen until you stop the car. The chaos in your life will remain just that until you decide that "enough is enough." Everything you are currently experiencing, you have the ability to change, redirect, and stop... If you choose to do so. The circumstances of your life are the way they are solely based on the fact that you are willing to tolerate them. This stop is critical for not only your future, but also your survival.

That day when Shawn asked me if I was okay, I came face to face with the reality that I had tolerated too much.

I had allowed myself to take the back seat in my life and allowed other people to drive. Rather than being the active participant, I chose—made the calculated decision—to be a bystander or part of the audience. My epiphany came when the tears wouldn't stop flowing, and I just broke. I chose to stop putting on the mask, to stop acting, to stop running from my problems, and face the music. So I did stop and make the necessary changes, and life for me started to change.

Shift

After you have stopped the car from crashing, it's time to shift, and position the car in a safe location.

Many of you are asking, what do you mean by shift? Shift can be defined in a number of different ways. One that stands out is "to put (something) aside and replace it with another or others; change or exchange." If we really want to be honest with ourselves, we can agree that most, if not all of our decisions have been based on our understanding of the environments and circumstances around us.

Some of us are willing and able to adjust more than others, while others are afraid to change. Some have created a comfort zone based on all the decisions they have made, and unfortunately are comfortable with useless information.

For those of us who are computer savvy, think back to the floppy disk. Everything done on the computer was saved on a floppy disk where you could retrieve it later if needed. With the evolution of time, the floppy disk has morphed into a flash drive. The flash drive is a better product to use to save your files. Having been continually modified to keep pace with the needs of the ever-changing computer, the flash drive has become a more effective, more resourceful, and more efficient way to save data. A necessary shift had to occur to keep up with the times. If the shift didn't happen, not only would the floppy disk become a relic, but so also would the computer. One essential element could affect a number of different parts in the long run.

The same can be said about shift that needs to happen in our minds, as it pertains to our philosophies. That thought that we are reluctant to change could be the one key we need to unlock our future. Let's reflect on the word obstacle for a moment. Many of us have grown to be apprehensive of obstacles, in some cases avoid them. To the average person, obstacles are "something material or nonmaterial that stands in the way of literal or figurative progress."

More or less it is considered to be a hindrance, a blockage, a hurdle. All of these things create a negative image in our minds, making us fearful of obstacles. With that understanding, obstacles become a platform for every possible excuse. We hear the word obstacle and associate it with a negative feeling, so we create an excuse to avoid the possible negative situation. Many have taken this road, because it is the one that requires the least amount of effort.

However, if we are looking to live a life above average, going through obstacles is the only way to begin the transformation process. The reason we are in our current circumstances is directly connected to how we view obstacles. For example, a single mother with children can say it is impossible for her to finish school and graduate college. Her excuse would be that she "has the kids." On the other hand, a woman with the same circumstance can say, "I have to finish school and graduate college because I have the kids." One chose to see the obstacle as a hindrance, while the other sees the same obstacle as a motivator, a reason to push through.

Business guru and philosopher Jim Rohn said, "Don't wish it were easier, wish you were better. Don't wish for less problems, wish for more skill. Don't wish for less challenges, wish for more wisdom." See, Mr. Rohn understood that once we changed our perspectives on the challenges of life, we would get better. The obstacle is only visible to magnify one of two things: your strength, or your weakness. Is it possible that the obstacle isn't the challenge, but the fear of exposure is the real issue?

In the movie *Coach Carter*, the head coach institutes a lock out, due to the poor grades of the players. While Coach Ken Carter is being interviewed, the players are off to the side having a conversation of their own. This conversation was centered on the fact that they knew some of the players had some challenges, but now the "world would know." That one factor sparked an argument amongst the players. As long as the obstacle was "their secret," it was okay. Once it became exposed, shame and disappointment became more important than the obstacle. If you would take a moment to watch the rest of the movie, you'd see that the players used the exposure to fuel their success. They made the resolve to overcome their challenges and defy all odds.

Show Up

Once you have taken the time to stop the car and shift your thinking, it's time to show up. Many will ask, what does it mean to show up? While many of us can agree that our lives are in a plot twist experience, some will not participate in their own rescue. We take the position that we will wait for someone to help us; we are afraid to be the most active part of the process. No one should be more invested in your change than you. No one else is living the pain you are going through, so you can't expect them to want it more than you. We have to stop the dependency on others to help us through *our* lives. Living with our hands out waiting for help only confirms the fact of your infant-like tendencies. This type of living shows that although we are "grown" and should be on solid foods, we're still on formula. We wonder why we are weak; however, we refuse to develop. We can't expect someone else to go to the gym for us, do all the workouts, and we get the muscles. At some point we have to get on the treadmill ourselves.

The first step to showing up is to take responsibility for where we are today. In his book *The Traveler's Gift,* Andy Andrews explains how one of the keys to transforming your life is to realize that "the buck stops here." No more will you put the blame for your current situation on anyone else but you. The reality is that whether people, places or things change, they don't impact your life. Complaining over spilled milk doesn't change the fact that the milk is spilled. Pointing fingers at everyone, assessing blame, complaining, diverting responsibility only prolongs the process. The very second we take the pacifier out of our mouths and actually grow up, we take control of our lives. We can't influence what other people do until we have a good handle on who we are and what we actually stand for. It's been said that life is 10% what actually happens and the other 90% is based on how we react to life. So let's leave these childish behaviors behind and show up.

Let's Recap:

1. Your only way to make a real resolution is to *Stop the Madness*. The car of your life is out of control, and the only person who can stop this crash is you. So stop the car.

2. Shift your thinking. Where you are is based on your old thinking; it's time to reboot and reprogram your computer. You need better updated software.

3. Show up for your rescue. Sending rescue efforts to an uninvited person is a waste of time and resources. No one should want your rescue more than you.

Chapter 3: Re-evaluate Your Associations

"A man only learns in two ways, one by reading, and the other by association with smarter people."
  – Will Rogers

Entertain this thought for a moment. You are given the opportunity to make a 180-degree change in your life, but it will be based on the circle of friends that you have now. What will that 180 degree change look like? Are you in a better place, or are you worse off than when you started? Are you living the lifestyle you have always imagined, or are you hating every waking moment that you live? Some will say it's really not that severe, but honestly, it is. Life serves as the best teacher. This is because it exposes all the good, bad, ugly, and indifferent that you tolerate. So if you are looking at life and it seems unfavorable, the first thing to evaluate is your philosophies, but even more importantly, your associations. It's been said that if you want the things around you to change, change the things around you. The current series of results you have been experiencing are directly correlated with the associations you have allowed. If you are looking for a complete 180-degree transformation, three basic principles have to be existent in order to be successful: disconnect from negative-minded people, determine that every connection going forward will push you to your destiny, and develop relationships that will stretch you.

Disconnect From Negative People

Too many times we make decisions and do things based on the people around us. We do everything based on what the group does. We live a life solely based on pleasing others and do everything based on how *they* think. Because we want to feel accepted, we allow others to dictate how we live our lives. If we take a hard look around, we can see the obvious results, honestly not looking good at all. One of the reasons you are reading this book is because you are looking for a 180 degree turn; you're tired of being stuck.

Let's start this process by doing something most hate, inspect what you expect. Look at the lifestyles of those in your current circle. Is it what you want for your future? Does it make you want what they have? Or is it the exact opposite? Are you cringing every time you see the effects of your choice? If none of your current associations produce fruit, you are existing in a morgue. Interestingly enough most hate being in a morgue; however, run their lives like one.

When you were younger you wanted so much more than what you have now, nothing was going to stop you. All of the friends you had wanted so much more out of their lives, and you joined with them and started to dream. As you got older your friends changed and so did your dreams. You lost touch with what really mattered. You didn't realize it, but you allowed your dreams to take a back seat. Suddenly you were accepting their norms and values, forgetting about your own. Until you looked in the mirror and saw the makings of a zombie.

See, every day when you were younger you would check in with your friends and see whose dreams were bigger. Some wanted to marry a sexy celebrity, others wanted to be a famous doctor or lawyer, and some wanted to become great athletes. One thing they had in common was they were all still big goals and dreams. Back then they would "watch" those who had what they wanted and mimic their every behavior. They inspected what they wanted and repeated it until that very behavior became second nature.

In the opening scene of the movie *Coach Carter*, coach Ken Carter, played by Samuel L. Jackson, comes to a game to see his old high school team play with the thought of getting the team into shape. Being a former basketball player who held records, he was able to observe and inspect the teams' strengths and weaknesses. Doing so gave him a full understanding of what he had to deal with before taking the position. If you are expecting to win, consider what improvements must be made in order for you to get that result.

Every good gardener knows that in order to have a flourishing garden, you have to pay attention and take care of what you have. You have to be vigilant and watch for weeds that will kill your garden. You have done all this work to till the ground, get the soil, find the right seed, watered the area to insure proper saturation, so the ground you have is fertile and ready for growth. The germination process begins, and you're excited when you see progress. Interestingly enough you go out one day and see weeds, but you overlook them and go on about your business as usual. That small error in judgment has now shifted the atmosphere of your garden.

I have been guilty of this same thing. I start making great strides towards a desired goal and allow a dream stealer to creep in and take residency in my life. At first it would be real subtle, they would joke about my success or lack thereof, and I would brush it off. See, what we tend to forget is that our minds are fertile ground, whatever we allow to exist in it will produce fruit, good or bad. So I would allow that poison to slowly creep in because I wasn't inspecting. It wasn't until I started noticing the effect that the poison was having on my garden that I reacted. By that time some damage was already done, I was already off track. Because I chose to ignore the venom when I heard it, I had to now stop and deal with the issues that were rising.

Most of us see the damage too late and just stop altogether and buy into the "junk mail." What I learned to do was "slow down to speed up." I realized that there was a challenge with my associations, course corrected and got right back on track. I learned that these dream stealers were only a distraction from the desired end result, so I either dealt with them by cutting them off or allowing them to take me off track. See, I have an appointment with destiny, I don't have time for any foolishness. If I allow you the opportunity to distract me, I will miss my destiny intersection—not going to happen. In my life exist two lanes: solutions and challenges, pick one. If you are a part of the solutions lanes let's plow ahead; however, if you are part of the challenges lane, you will get left behind.

Develop A Mastermind Team

Once you have taken the time to differentiate between dream stealers and dream builders, it's time to develop a mastermind team. Right now it seems like your team is exactly what you need, but is that really true? They are always doing the same things; however, you want better. They live a life of entitlement, they have no drive, they are lazy in all that they do, and they attempt to live the life of what they see. But you actually want bigger and better. At one point you have to see that the life you live is based on the associations pulling and pushing you. If everyone in your circle is looking to you for advice, you are in the wrong circle. In each area of your life you have to have someone stretching you past your potential. Seeing what you want is one thing; however, creating the environment that will produce what you want is where you will find most of the challenge.

Isn't it funny how we see the person with the amazing physique and want what they have. Our eyes get enlarged, our hearts race, we grow a desire. Some of us actually go out and buy the outfits, sneakers, and memberships, all just to look like we are doing something. The appearance is great; however, the one thing we lack is a coach. Many will say that they don't need a coach to get the physique, they already know what to do. If you did, you would have the physique you desire. What we fail to understand is that the one with the extraordinary physique applied a series of disciplines that produced a result.

My bishop says that discipline is "enforced obedience." Are you willing to enforce a series of obedient actions? One of the reasons to have a mastermind team is because they will push you to "enforce" the needed obedience to get your result. If you have ever watched weight lifters work out together, you've seen how they push each other. Throughout all the grunts and growls, they will not let each other off the hook until the rep is done. Who in your circle is pushing you that hard? If no one in your current team is doing that for you, it's time to change your team. As you look to change the mastermind team, make sure you are reaching past where you are.

Too many times we look to get help from those who are exactly where we are. Oscar Wilde said, "Most people are other people. Their thoughts are someone else's opinions, their lives a mimicry, their passions a quotation." We take valuable time listening to the opinions of people who aren't living their own lives. Because we are looking to be accepted by a group of people, we ignore the fact that they don't have one iota of what we want. They have zero manifestation of what we want for our lives, yet because they recognize us, we adopt their opinions.

What we fail to remember is that opinions produce thoughts, thoughts produce actions, actions produce habits and habits produce lifestyle. So if we mindlessly negotiate the lifestyle that we want for the opinions of those who don't have what we want, we forfeit the right to complain. We willingly allow someone else's average opinion to become the GPS of our lives, while we pout because it's not what we want. So before anyone gets the privilege to rent space in your life, make sure they possess the lifestyle you want and push you past your potential.

You have to be willing to be the general contractor to the architect of your strategy. Once the plan is out into the atmosphere, it waits for you to give it life. This is like a designer putting together an elegant gown with intricate details but having no one to bring it to life. The designer needs to have a willing and able body to make the gown live. You are that body. Your willingness, desire to put in work, your hunger to make this time different, your I-won't-be-denied mindset is what makes the plan work.

Develop Tough Skin

Too many times we say we want a glamorous lifestyle; however, we have baby soft skin. Anything someone says or does offends us, and we run away. I have learned from my bishop that offense is a choice. None of us in this world is perfect, so we are not without reproach. As you look to change your mastermind team, make an effort to find those who will not co-sign your mess. We have to look for the ones who will not only applaud our successes, but also prick you when you are out of line. What happens is we see the shine of things and think they're easy to obtain.

Life will bring you to an awakening moment when you find

that dreams require work. In the movie *Coach Carter*, Timo Cruz thought he had everything he needed to be successful in life. He was a gangster selling drugs and found his way on the basketball team. Timo thought that anyone who challenged him would be dealt with severely. What Timo didn't realize was that Coach Ken Carter was exactly what he needed. Coach was hard-nosed, straight to the point, he made you work for what you wanted.

Isn't it interesting that we want the finer things in life; however, we want the shortcut, microwave way to get it. Not only do we want the microwaved shortcut, we want the expert helping us to have pity on us and make it easy. Somehow we think we get a lottery ticket and just win, but no… reality requires you to put some work in to get true results. So finding a mastermind team that will take no excuses is critical. But more importantly we can't have a woe is me attitude. Life will not take it easy on you, so having a team that will make you dig deep is necessary.

Life has an interesting way of teaching us a lesson when we refuse to have the necessary discipline to get the job done. In the same movie *Coach Carter*, Timo Cruz comes back begging to get back on the team. He realized that he needed to be part of the team; more importantly, he realized what he was doing wasn't working. Before he was able to make it back on the team, he had to pay a "re-entry price" which was 2500 push-ups and 1000 suicides. Timo wasn't just going to be allowed back on the team, and life will not just allow you to get back on the horse and ride. You have to now pay the prerequisite to get back in. The only way to do that is to have the rhino skin. The old things can't bother you as much because now you're looking to make this the last time you're at rock bottom. So your mastermind team has to be strong enough not to give in to your crying but must push you.

As the movie *Coach Carter* progresses, we find Timo Cruz at the deadline, where his prerequisites are due for his re-entry, but he hasn't accomplished the mission. Now you would think that Coach would let him back on for the little that he has left, but he doesn't. Coach Carter actually tells him to leave the gym. Some will say that was cruel; however, it's the response of the team that makes the major difference. Now he had 1000 suicides, of which he had 80 left and 2500 push-ups of which he had 500 left. His teammates decided to help him finish; they chose to do some for him. See the team will push you when you think you have nothing left in the tank.

They will help you develop that rhino skin where nothing distracts you from your goal. They will force you to face the music; however, you will not be alone.

Let's Recap:

Since you are looking to make this your final at-Rock-Bottom experience, you will need to re-evaluate your associations in the following ways:

1. Disconnect from negative people. Allowing negative people to remain in your life will prolong your recovery process. Disconnecting gives you a chance to deal with obstacles, make changes, and grow.

2. Develop a Mastermind Team. You can't do this comeback alone. You're going to need a team of people around you who are better than you in all areas. They will pull you up and stretch you past your potential. They will make you allergic to being average.

3. Develop tough skin. This rebirth of you is not for the faint of heart. You're going to have to grow up and face the challenges. The baby tender skin won't cut it at this level. You're going to have to "toughen up, buttercup."

Chapter 4: Remove the Doubt

"Doubt kills more dreams than failure ever will."
— Anonymous

So you have done everything you know to do and failed. You put everything behind this project and it just didn't work. You fought long and hard for your marriage to work, but it just fell apart. You made all these promises because it was a sure thing, and it all tanked. We have all been in this place in life at one point in time. That feeling in the pit of your stomach where you are embarrassed because all your hard work went down the drain. Most of us who get to this place come to a fork in the road where we have to make a decision: Do I take another shot at this or do I close up shop and quit?

What Is Your Why?

Unfortunately, most of us quit and start a habit of quitting. We allow the disappointment of failing to overshadow the reason why we started in the first place. This is where doubt creeps in and starts to grow roots in our lives. Many definitions exist for the word doubt; however, one stands out the most, "to be uncertain about something, be undecided in opinion or belief." This is where most of us get paralysed and just stop everything. We analyze everything: every mistake, every decision, every thought, everything associated with the failure. We double check and triple check because we are just not sure.

One of the biggest challenges I have had with doubt was not having a strong enough "why" to keep me going through the hard times. Most of what I started was because someone else was doing it; I just hopped on the bandwagon. It's been said that your "why" should be strong enough to make you cry, should keep you up at night, should stir up emotions that push you when you really want to quit. Your why is that one thing that will reinvigorate you when everything around you is crumbling.

See, that rock bottom experience is one where we allowed life to beat us up over and over, making us numb to anything that will change our condition. We have become so numb by the frostbite of life that we feel nothing, and we find it okay to fall back into the average lifestyle. The interesting thing about frostbite is that it burns and is very painful at first; however, the longer it remains it becomes numb. Now this numbness is to the point of actually having to cut that body part off. So we have conditioned ourselves to become so numb that we cut off our dreams, goals, aspirations because we just didn't have a strong enough why.

My mentor, Darnell Self explained a story where he was teaching on having a strong why, and he asked a gentleman to share his why. The gentleman said that he needed to bring in a certain amount of money a year. My mentor asked, "But why?" The gentleman replied, "To buy a house for my kids." Again my mentor asked, "But why?" The gentleman replied, "So that my kids can have their own rooms." My mentor then said, "I'm going to challenge you to be more specific, and then asked, "But why?" The gentleman became a bit emotional as he said, "I have two boys and a girl, and they share a room. As my daughter is getting older, she wants her own space, so she asks from time to time, 'Daddy when will I be in my own room?' And I keep saying soon. Sometimes I have to turn away, in order to fight back the emotion and tears because I am tired of saying soon." My mentor then says, "That's your why."

Until you make your why that personal, that specific, that real, you will quit at every intersection of challenge. See, before any major building is built, time is spent on building the foundation necessary to uphold the height of the building. Your why has to become the foundation that will hold you up and help you weather the storms.

As you start working towards your why, you will find that it may need to be adjusted, tweaked. That is perfectly fine. It's been said that a rocket is off course 97% of the time, along the way it's programmed to make course corrections and adjustments to ensure proper landing on the target. Like the rocket, you will do the same, that is if it is your intention to hit your goal. One thing is for certain, life will always happen, and as it does we can make one of two choices: to react or to respond.

Let's consider your sense of vision. Many of us start life with perfect 20/20 vision; however, as time and age progress, our ability to see becomes challenged. So we go to the eye doctor to make the adjustments necessary to see. In most cases the doctor will give us a prescription to get glasses. Those glasses have been measured to fit and correct our challenges. What many of us do is make the investment to purchase the glasses to correct our vision. We wear the glasses for a short while, and see little to no change, so we stop wearing them. What we fail to realize is that our vision became impaired over a period of time. So adjustments may have to be made to correct our impairment. Rather than reacting negatively and saying the heck with these annoying glasses, and not wearing them, we should take them back to the specialist for correction. The longer we sit in our self-pity mentality, the longer it will take for us to get back on track.

Trust In You

Along with your why, you have to trust in yourself. Too many times we second guess our own internal "gut instincts." We start out with a dream, put some goals behind it, gather supporting evidence, and we are ready to launch into the deep. Somewhere along the way we get cold feet, we get the butterflies in our stomach, and we start to doubt. Regardless of how great that dream was, we shrink back as if it never existed. We face a hurdle and fail at it the first time, then we throw our hands up. Somewhere, in our minds we thought because we came up with it, it was supposed to be easy. Wherever we saw the hurdle, we think that it must not have been the right plan for me. We lose our grind because we are faced with a brick wall that challenges us. This is where we have to decide to either turn on the switch or leave it off.

I'm reminded of the movie series *The Fast and the Furious*. In this series a group of individual's street race to show whose car is better. They take the time to make the necessary adjustments to their cars to give them the fighting edge. One particular feature is the addition of nitrous oxide system, also known as NOS. Once the button was pushed to activate the NOS, the car would push past its normal limitations and accelerate at a hyper speed. What was interesting was that the NOS wasn't automatic, it required the driver to push the button. This is where most drivers win or lose. The experienced drivers knew with confidence exactly at what point to hit the switch. The driver had practiced this several times to get to a comfortable place. Like the driver, you have to be willing to practice, drill, and rehearse until you get it right. It's not all going to happen in one shot. Not only do you have to trust the process, you have to trust yourself.

Most experienced drivers were horrible when they started; however, they were willing to continue to practice over and over until they got it right. That confidence will come, but you will never know until you believe in yourself, and your efforts. Will you make mistakes? Sure you will. However, those mistakes help eliminate the wrong possibilities, and get you close to the right one. If you choose to quit, you may be one attempt away from getting it right. In the movie *Remember the Titans*, two sets of players, Caucasians and African Americans, were fighting to show who was superior. The challenge was they were on the same team. It wasn't until they believed in each other that they won as a team. They had to practice over and over to synchronize their abilities, to grow that confidence in each other. Their plays had to become instinctual.

In the same way you have a goal, a plan of action; however, they are not synchronized. This is where you keep grinding, pushing and believing in you. Your efforts are only in vain *if you stop*. Driving in the vehicle of life you gain momentum, that momentum only works if you continue to push the accelerator. The moment you stop pushing the vehicle, your goals, along with the plan of action, slow down. The only way to get back to where you were, is to apply twice the effort, because you have lost momentum.

Most will quit when it doesn't go right the first time, not realizing how ridiculous that is. That's like getting one flat tire, then popping the other three. While this sounds silly, we all have been guilty of doing this at one point or another. We didn't get the job, they turned us down, we failed a class; whatever it is, that disappointment hurts. That pain makes us lose confidence in ourselves, saying, "Maybe this wasn't for me." Nothing could be further from the truth. You have ventured off into the deep, into uncharted waters with a tug boat. The interesting part is that you may need to tweak some things and may not be that far off. You've fallen, but you *can* get up. Dust yourself off and get back to it...**YOU GOT THIS!**

By now you have refocused your why and reignited your trust in yourself—now it's time to make an impression. Too long have you ridden on someone else's coattails, relied on everyone else's perspective to design your future. Your time is now. Your belief in you has to be far greater than that of anyone else.

Let's remember that the movie of your life has you in the leading role, no one can be you better than you. Consider this for a moment:

Identical twins born in the same womb, while having similar physical features, are different. If we look at the face, body, and even mannerisms, they mimic each other. But let's look a little deeper. Let's observe their fingerprints.

A number of different definitions exist for the word fingerprint; however, the one that stands out the most is "an impression of the markings of the inner surface of the last joint of the thumb or other fingers." These impressions are unique to a specific individual, not a family, society, region—a person. Your life is like your fingerprint. While similar impressions and markings may exist, yours were custom made and tailored to you and you alone. This is why crime scene investigators take their time to evaluate a scene. They know that if they find a fingerprint, it narrows their search because no two fingerprints are the same. This is why trusting in you is so vitally important. I am not suggesting you should discount the advice of others, what I am saying is that you should make your instinct the foundation of you and build on that.

Seek wise counsel, but never discount your perspective.

Your voice and thoughts not only matter, they are the nourishment someone else needs to survive. I have this saying "There's nothing new under the sun but a new day," meaning your situation is unique to you, but has happened before. The one component that has changed is you, so that is what makes it as unique as the fingerprint. Don't be afraid to make your impression, even if it requires repetition.

Let's consider yet another perspective. When you go to a movie, you choose it because of the commercials, recommendations from friends, and more importantly, experience you've had watching a particular actor/actress playing a role. That particular person, for you, brings the movie alive. Without them the movie would've flopped. Let's evaluate two of these actors: Vin Diesel and Denzel Washington.

Vin Diesel has been made famous for a number of movies; however, one stands out above the rest, *The Fast and the Furious* series. After you watched the first one, which was action packed and had you on the edge of your seat, you expected the same in the movies to come. Vin Diesel has never disappointed in any of those movies. It is as if they custom made the movie for him.

The interesting part of this is that every actor/actress brought into the movie became better the more they would interact with Diesel.

With every movie made after the first, you anticipated the same if not better. Denzel Washington has the same effect on the movies when he's had the lead role. Consider movies like *Malcom X, Hurricane, American Gangster,* and *Fences.* In each of these roles, Washington made you believe he was the actual person he was scripted to be. He embodied every aspect of the person. He studies them down to a science. So when he plays the role you are drawn to believe.

The same has to be said for you. The role you play in the movie of your life is the leading one, not a supporting actor/actress. You have given the starring role to others for too long, and they have caused your movie to flop. Your movie. The movie that you have spent so much time thinking through, living, being, and you have allowed them to give you a back seat? You wanted greatness, you wanted to change the legacy of your family, you wanted to live differently, or were those just interesting suggestions? No longer can you sit by and allow *your* life to be written by anyone else but you. Stand up and make this movie what you want it to be, create the plot twist that shocks the world, be the reason why someone gets up again and lives.

We minimize our stories because we think they are insignificant; however, someone is looking at you and saying to themselves, "How is it possible that they can still smile?" Your playing small serves no purpose to you or your audience. Yes, they are watching how you respond to the jabs of life. They are waiting to see the magnificence that comes from you. Will you rise, or will you fall? The choice is yours.

Take The First Step

Sounds really simple, but for most of us it isn't. Regardless of how well-crafted the plan may be, how deep and tear jerking your why could be, without that first step, it will remain just that, a thought. It is said that the most expensive place in the world is a graveyard. That's because millions have died with goals, dreams, and aspirations that remained in their minds, and never manifested. Those who could have cured cancer, been the President of the United States, a philanthropist, or who knows what else. The one thing that we know is we will never know. The same will be for you. If you don't get up from your rock bottom, the world will never know you.

Have you ever been in a place where you heard and/or saw something that you were considering? "I was just thinking of that," is what you said when you delayed yourself from taking the first step. My mentor, coach, spiritual mom, Pastor Monica Haskell always says, "History has been made of firsts, but that first started with a first step." You may be thinking that it's been done already by those who are better than you. That may be true; however, they are not you. You bring a uniqueness to the table that no one else can. Your presence, perspective, and perception are all that make your approach different.

I have learned a couple of lessons from those who most would overlook. Many times society looks for solutions from the perceived elite; however, some of the best lessons are learned from those who are considered lowly. In the movie *A Family that Preys*, a disheveled man comes to the diner, day in and day out. The owners of the diner care for him, despite his outward appearance. These same owners run into a challenge, and they need help to come out of it. It was the disheveled one, who was down on his luck, who helped them out. See, that same disheveled man was one of the most brilliant minds as it pertained to finances. So many overlooked, ridiculed, harassed, and even made him feel less of a man. How many times have we allowed others to speak into our lives, making deposits into the good soil of our lives. The longer we allow them to make deposits, the fruit will start to germinate.

However, if we are the first to take the step, plant the seed, make the impression, the rest will have to play second to you. Lao Tzu has been quoted as saying, "The journey of a thousand miles starts with one step." Now that you are no longer falling, and are on your feet, take the first step to the new you. See, that first step is so critical that we celebrate when a child takes their first step. For a while they are on their bellies, depending on someone else to carry them, do for them. As they get to their feet, and often wobble and most times fall, they are gaining confidence. They are learning to trust their legs until they stand. They now have to move their feet, a new adventure for them. Up to this point they were handicapped by those who carried them for so long. They now have to learn the mechanics of moving their feet. In the process they will stumble, millions of times; however, eventually they master the first step.

Up to this point you have been given the basic mechanics to start your journey, but it's the application of these mechanics that make this first step so critical. This first step is the door opening to your new future. That first step is followed by another and yet another, releasing you from the dependency of another. Whether it's sobriety, abstinence, starting your own business, finishing school; whatever it is, they all start with the first step. Be bold, take that first step and watch how the world opens up to you. Will you wobble? Will you fall? Sure, that's where you learn what didn't work and do it again. The beauty of the first is that a second, third, and fourth will follow and that, my friend, is where you just take off like a rocket.

Let's Recap:

While we may have the ingredients to the new you, nothing happens until we remove all obstructions, including doubt. We do that by performing the following steps:

1. Revisit your why. Focus on the reason you started this journey. Reevaluate and make it a reason that will move you to action, no matter what you're facing. Your why has to be strong enough to make you emotional and even cry.

2. Trust yourself. You've trusted everything and everyone else up to this point and it hasn't worked. Why not take a chance on yourself? Make the mark that only you can make.

3. Don't be afraid to take the first step. You've been conditioned to believe that it wasn't for you, or that it's too hard, or that you're not worthy. Yes, you are. Let's take that first step back to the new you.

Chapter 5: Retire Your Past

"Your past cannot be changed. The future is yet in your power."
– Unknown

We have looked at a number of strategies and principles up to this point; however, nothing is more important than retiring your past. Two concepts stand out in this process, that of retiring, and that of the past. Many definitions exist for the word retire, but the one that fits this process is "to remove from active service, or usual field of activity." Now let's consider the word past: "an earlier period of a person's life, career, etc., that is thought to be shameful or of an embarrassing nature." So, if we take these two expanded definitions and combine them, here is what it could sound like "the process by which one removes shameful and embarrassing periods of their life, career, etc., from active service."

Wow, imagine if we really did that? If we made a calculated decision to put our past into retirement, drew a line in the sand, and started over. That would be the ultimate reset. However, many of us find ourselves wrapped in our past to the point where we paralyse ourselves. We create an orchestra of music playing the amazing tune of "woe is me." The interesting part of the past is that it has already happened and can't be changed. We have played this tune so much we have purchased each instrument, mastered them, and play them all simultaneously. While that picture seems ridiculous, many of us live that daily. We've initiated an all-out war against ourselves, and yes, we have made ourselves enemy number one. Our past has forgiven us of the shortcomings and failures, yet we want them to hold us hostage.

Only The Foundation

Every major building has a foundation. Whether it's a skyscraper or a residential mansion, they all need a strong, sturdy foundation. Without it the edifice will never stand. The interesting part is that the foundation provides the roots, or depth of the structure; it is what's above the foundation that is recognized. While being an important part of the process, it is just that—a part. If we take an even deeper look at the word foundation and its definition, we find it to be "the basis or groundwork of anything." If we parallel this definition to our lives, we can see how the foundation plays a role; however, is not *the* role.

Let's look at the movie *Stomp the Yard*. Theta Nu Theta had an amazing base, they created a platform where the fraternity was doing very well; however, they lost their flare when it came to the step competition. They were expecting to win with old outdated routines, while other fraternities were evolving. Before we delve into this next phase, let me say that the veterans were taught well; their formations were intact, their synchronization was intact; however, it was old. As the movie continues, we find DJ, a Neo, as he is considered, challenging the veterans. The two squads battle, and the veterans win. See, that was just it, they won against newcomers, but would always lose the competition. It wasn't until they retired the regiment of the old, combined their base to the passion and flare of the Neos, that they won the competition.

The same can be said about our lives. Until we retire the past, we will be stuck in two worlds, never moving forward. I'm not saying that the foundation isn't necessary; it is needed. Jack Scalia was quoted as saying, "…because if you have a strong foundation like we have, you can build or rebuild anything on it. But if you've got a weak foundation you can't build anything." Realize he didn't say you can try to build, he said you can't build anything. So life is being held hostage because we can't move from the past? The key to the new you is in your pocket, yet you willfully choose not to use it.

If you are serious about the pain you feel, draft the papers for retirement, turn them in and move forward. I say this because until the leader of the Theta Nu Theta fraternity embraced it, they would continue to lose. You can't spend the rest of your life looking in the rearview mirror, wondering why you're not moving forward. Did they abandon you, hurt you, betray you? Did you fail? Yes. That was only training, it was the one thing that once you mastered life, would never be the same, unless you like it at rock bottom.

Push Past The Benchmark

While the past is a foundation, it also serves as a benchmark. Your past was a sequence of events that framed the person you are today. When you look in the mirror you see the reflection of everything you have been through. In many cases we see the truth that most will never see. We do an amazing job of disguising the scars and acting as if we are invincible. The reality is that those scars serve as a reminder of a time when everything we believed was challenged. These moments were breaking points where we pushed past the blood, sweat, and tears…and survived. Some of us; however, don't bounce back. Rather than driving through the intersection of our past, we park and stay in that one spot.

Traffic is piling up behind us, yet we stay parked. We allow the impasse to be our permanent resting place. Rather than it being a benchmark, we make it our home.

Before we move past this point, let's take a moment to understand what the benchmark really represents. One definition that stands out is "any standard or reference by which others can be measured or judged." Let's consider this point for a minute. At a certain time in history, it was said that it was impossible to run a mile in four minutes. That was a benchmark. It was until Roger Bannister ran the mile in 3:59.4. Prior to Banister it was considered out of the question; that was their benchmark. It's been said that Bannister's time served as the new benchmark and has since been broken. The benchmark is now 3:43.13. While Bannister astonished the world with his accomplishments, the world of track and field didn't just leave it at that, they created a new benchmark.

Your life is the same way. Benchmarks have been set by generations before you. They understood the standard but created new ones. Was it challenging? Yes, however, that is what creates that positive flow in your life. Whatever happened in your life prior to this book was just a benchmark, it was what you needed to endure to get you here. The real question is what do you do now? Both Coach Carter and Coach Boone were faced with a standard; however, they knew they were facing a losing battle, and something had to change quickly. Losing wasn't an option; they had to push past their benchmarks in order to win. In the same way, we have to look at any benchmark as an opportunity to push past what we consider limitations, we have to dig deeper. Your greatest accomplishments come after you have faced the challenging benchmark set before and overcome it. That benchmark is just a test to justify if you qualify for what you want.

Redefine You

As a photographer, I have taken thousands if not millions of pictures. When I go back and start the editing process, I sometimes ask myself, "What were you thinking?" This is because the shot was horrible, no focus, heads chopped off, just a disaster. I could've easily said, "I'm not good enough" and quit. But what would that prove? Would it say I couldn't handle the simple task of taking a picture? I should sell my equipment and find another hobby? To some this would sound ridiculous; however, that is how many of us live our lives. We walk around on eggshells, praying that we never make a mistake. The interesting part of it all is that the mistakes give you a chance to perfect your skill. The more I took the time to practice, to apply what I learned from my mistakes, the better I became. Even where I am now in photography, I know that I have not yet arrived. I am always looking to get better, always looking to redefine what people thought they knew of me.

Because you find yourself in the rock bottom phase, momentum upward will be recognized. In the movie *The Karate Kid*, Daniel Laruso was the new guy in town being bullied by the high school jocks. It wasn't until he was sick and tired of the humiliation, got nearly beaten to death, and got rescued by Mr. Miyagi, did he look to redefine himself. Daniel knew something had to change, and he had to do something drastic. So he asked Mr. Miyagi to teach him how to fight. In the same manner life has given you blow after blow after blow, and you're just tired of the punishment. This is where you gather every last fiber of your being and launch into the new you. You look for help to make you better. You make the drastic changes necessary to let the world know "the buck stops here."

To better understand this concept of redefine let's look at its definition. The one that stands out is "to give new meaning to.

" So Daniel had to give a new meaning to what people thought of him. He had to make the necessary changes to insure the change was real. The interesting part of his redefinition process was that it wasn't what he expected. Sometimes your breakthrough is packaged differently from what you expect it to be. See, to redefine means you are giving a new meaning to something, the new you. So you can't use old tactics for a new level. Each level requires a new set of skills, philosophies, and wisdom. Where you are now is directly tied to the decisions you have made over the last five years. If you are looking for this rock bottom launch to be different, you're going to have to get a new sheet of paper and rework this plan. No more can you even take the time to consider the old way. This is the new you, time to make this the last time you are ever in this position. No more firecracker launches, this launch has to be like a rocket taking off, it is a life-altering experience.

Let's Recap:

We all have a past; it is what initiates our journey. However, holding on to that view in the rearview mirror leads us to not only lose sight of what's ahead, but it also compromises the future of those around us. Here's how we prevent that from happening:

1. Realize the past is only a foundation. Once you are born you are living in the present. You're now growing backward you're evolving into being relevant or a relic.

2. Your past is a benchmark. It can be where you sit and watch life pass you by, or a starting block to the race of your life. Because life continues to move, you have to do the same and start your race.

3. Now that you are here at rock bottom, redefine yourself. Make this surge to greatness worth every breath that you take. Your pain is real, make it worth something. Tell yourself what my mentor Pastor Monica Haskell says, "If it looks like I am losing, it's only halftime."

Chapter 6: Relinquish Your Ego

"The ego is the single biggest obstruction to achievement of anything."

– Richard Rose

This journey that you are taking back to the new and improved you has been an interesting one. We have learned a great deal up to this point; however, just like baking a cake, all the ingredients have to be present. One we haven't discussed is the challenge of your ego. It's that one ingredient that will either accelerate or destroy your transformation process. Before we move any further, let's understand what your ego actually is. Ego "is the idea or opinion that you have of yourself, esp. the level of your ability and intelligence, and your importance as a person."

Too many times we look at ourselves through distorted lenses and think more of ourselves than is actually there. I am speaking past the level of confidence; this is shifting into an air of being conceited. This puts us in a comprising position because we believe no one can share with us a different perspective, no one can teach us anything, we have the final say and that is it. While we are in this rock bottom space we have to relinquish our egos if we are really looking to change our lives' outcomes.

When we learn to relinquish our egos, we are choosing to let them go or releasing them. For many of us this is a hard thing to do; we'd rather hold on to what hasn't worked this far.

Let Go The Pride

Whenever I have heard the conversations regarding ego, pride has been one of the first things mentioned. I've heard, "I can't stand them, they have so much pride they won't ask for help." You're drowning in your pride, dying by the second, but you won't ask for help. That is like having cancer, the doctor has your treatment, but you make the calculated decision not to take it. You'd rather die than take the help that will save you. I'm sorry but that makes absolutely no sense; however, some of us live that scenario daily. Our pride has imprisoned us, but we have the key in our pocket to get out.

C.S. Lewis once said, "A proud man is always looking down on things and people; and, of course, as long as you are looking down, you cannot see something that is above you." Wow! You'd rather walk around hunched over than upright. You'd rather spend your time looking at the ground, bumping into things, falling, getting lost. You then have the audacity to be upset when you fall. In the movie the *Pursuit of Happiness*, John Gardener's wife is fed up with the way their lives have been, and she wants out. She decides that she wants to take their son with her. At that exact moment John Gardner has one of two choices to make: beat his chest and stand behind his pride justifying everything or humble himself and grind. The reality was whatever he chose to do, he would endure some pain and challenges. If you're going to have to deal with pain, make it worth something, believe that it is not just pain.

In the movie *Coach Carter*, Timo Cruz allowed his pride to get the best of him; he didn't think he needed Coach Ken Carter. As the movie progresses, you can see that Timo wants to come back, but he allows his pride to hold him back. It was not until his cousin got shot that he realized he needed the coach more than the coach needed him. Isn't it interesting that the place he least expected to help him was exactly what shifted his life? How many times have we missed destiny moments because of our pride? Unlike Cruz, we may not have a second chance to get it right. The fact that you are reading this book is a clear indication that you know your life has to change. Don't make this just another read. Throw your pride out the window and take this journey to the new you.

Faith

The second level of relinquishing your ego is to have faith that you're going to conquer your current situation. Rodney, you have no idea what I am facing, faith isn't going to get me out of this. Really? So you've tried everything up to this point, nothing has worked, and you're going to lie here in the fetal position and allow life to beat you? You're willing to lose? Many of us say we have faith; however, it is just a word we heard someone else use that sounded good. We heard our grandmother use it over and over again not realizing the magnitude of the word. You see, faith is that one ingredient that shifts the atmosphere of everything in your life. You can almost say that faith is the yeast that your life needs to rise.

I've been known to dabble in cooking and have heard that I know what I am doing in that arena; however, when it comes to baking, I am a novice. Baking is the science that requires you to be exact in your measurements if you want what you are making to come out right. Baking deals with specifics, while cooking deals with your particular taste. This is why most of us are frustrated with life because we are using cooking knowledge on a baking experience. While the principles and concepts seem the same, they are not. See in cooking, you can adjust as you go; however, in baking you're restricted to specifics. In cooking, you can add ingredients on the front or back end of the process.

One of the ingredients that is crucial in baking is yeast. Yeast is a kind of fungus that is used to make bread rise. Yeast is also defined as something that causes fermentation or agitation. Is it possible that the reason you are in the rock bottom phase, is because you are or haven't been agitated enough to rise? This ingredient is so important it's incorporated into flour and sold as self-rising flour. If we take away this leavening ingredient, the baked goods will not be the same. Have you ever had bread with no yeast? It is flat, it is unidimensional, it lacks depth. This is sometimes how we choose to live life. While we have the potential to rise, we choose to live life flat. The interesting part of this agitating process is that the only way to add it is to start all over. Which is why rock bottom is not a bad place to be right now. You can dump the old batter and start all over with all the necessary ingredients.

Many may know that I am a New England Patriots fan. One of the reasons why I love this team is because of the amazing leadership of the quarterback, Tom Brady. While most hate him,

I have to say that he is one of the best leaders that has ever played the game. Time and time again he has been tested and has come out on top. For the football fans, consider for a moment the Super Bowl LI, the New England Patriots versus the Atlanta Falcons. As everyone watched in amazement, the game was set. Towards the end of the third quarter, the score was Falcons - 28 and the Patriots - 3. I believe the world was ready to call it over. Falcons fans were already celebrating, but Tom Brady and the Patriots had other plans.

The yeast, the leavening ingredient, the agitating component became activated. The Patriots scored a field goal, making the score Falcons - 28 and Patriots - 6. To many who were watching, the game was over going into the fourth quarter. Brady and the Patriots remained poised, making play after play, moving the needle. The Patriots eventually tied the game and went into overtime. To many who were watching, that within itself was amazing; however, it wasn't good enough. See, Tom Brady and the Patriots had come too far. All the odds were stacked against them to make it this far, they were not supposed to win. Their faith was being tested, and there could only be one outcome, either you win, or you lose. Brady knew that they had worked too hard to lose.

Many of you are facing the same challenges. Life has "checked your chin" one time too many. The interesting thing is that you have defied all odds and are still here. Or maybe they are all expecting you to fail, and it looks like you just might. This is where your faith kicks in, that switch is flipped, and you push past. This is where you put your ego aside and dig deep. This is where you count on that yeast to rise. If you have ever watched bread being made, you know that the dough can be made with the yeast added; however, until it is put into the oven and heat is added, it won't rise. Another interesting fact is that the bread doesn't rise instantly, the oven has to be a certain temperature.

Many of you were right on course for the yeast to kick in, but you thought it was taking too long, so you quit. You opened the oven too early. Now your bread has to sit in the oven longer. See, this faith thing is a process. It won't happen overnight; you have to work at it. You have to be willing to take the heat just a little while longer. For some of you, your IQ level is too low. When I say IQ, I'm referring to your I Quit level. Your faith has to have the I Will Until attitude. Quitting is not an option.

The New England Patriots ended up winning the Super Bowl 34 to 28. Please take note: not only did the Patriots win, but the Falcons never scored again. Once your faith kicks in, your ego has to take a seat. Nothing else matters. You don't quit until you win. It's been said, "When the going gets tough, the tough get going." How tough are you willing to be to win? How far are you willing to go to win? What sacrifices are you willing to make to be in your end zone? Life will not stop moving just because you do. So move with it. Make the course corrections along the way, boost your IQ level, and know losing is never an option. Let the world know, "If it looks like I am losing, it's only halftime." Come out of the locker room with the confidence that "I Win."

Get Over Yourself

Humble pie is a pastry that many of us have had the unfortunate privilege of tasting. At one point or another our ego causes us to build this nonexistent world where we are always right. We live in this bubble and believe nothing outside the four corners of our minds matters. Some of us learn quickly that we're not as mighty as we thought we were.

I have to say that I have had healthy helpings of humble pie, more times than I want to admit. One in particular stands out. I was a freshman in college, and up to that point I had done pretty well academically. I lived in a strict home, so this was my chance to spread my wings, or so I thought. I began making decisions—because I thought I was grown—that later had consequences I never saw coming. Many of us live life and come to a crossroad, where we feel that we have arrived. We think because of education, experience, or now new circles, that we are untouchable. For me it was an argument with my parents, that led me to think, *why won't they just let me live my life?* As my parents they were giving me some advice that contradicted what I wanted. So one night after a huge argument, I decided to leave. I thought, *That's enough, I'll show them.*

For a while all was going well, I was living the life. Everything was good until I hit a brick wall. The life I thought was peaches and cream, changed on a dime. Everything came tumbling down, and I had nowhere to turn. I had to go back to the place I promised myself I would never return to and ask for help.

My ego wasn't in my back pocket; it was under my feet. I had to get over the fact that they were right, and I was wrong. If I wanted to make it through, I had to let it all go. Yes, I heard the, "I told you so," but it's what I had to hear because I was so hard headed.

If you are serious about this comeback, you have to let some things go. Your very existence is associated with just letting go. Even at this point in my life I am still learning to let go. We hold on to things for so long we cause our own paralysis—spiritually, physically, emotionally, and socially. We would recover so much faster if we'd just learn to let go. We delay our appointment with destiny because we won't allow the pain and the hurt to teach us, and then move past it. Give yourself a chance to live by releasing the emergency brake, and letting your car go.

Let's Recap:

All the ingredients necessary for your life to change can be present; however, if you don't make the calculated decision to relinquish your ego, it will be just another unaccomplished goal. You can relinquish your ego by

1. Letting go of pride. This is when you realize that you have made a mistake, and you may need help to fix it. It is where you understand that you are human, and yes, it is okay to reach out for help.

2. Apply your faith. Many times people are egotistical because they are embarrassed. They don't want anyone to know that they messed up, or that they lost their way. So they put up a façade that shows they knew what they were doing all along, when in reality they lost their faith. Have faith, know that it takes time to get your goals accomplished, and know that it's all worth it in the end.

3. Get over yourself. Too many times our arrogance makes it hard for people to approach us. Humility will take you a long way. It's okay, mistakes happen; how you respond to them is what really matters. Stay humble.

Chapter 7:   Refuse to Ever Be in This Position Again

"Success in life comes when you simply refuse to give up, with
goals so strong that obstacles, failures, and loss act as
motivation…"

– Anonymous

The first six principles were all amazing and critical in your journey back to the new you. They lay a blueprint needed to recreate a once-destroyed person. Like all new construction of high rises, the architect embraces the vision of its owner; however, it is the expert contractor who executes the masterpiece to perfection. What is interesting in this new construction is that not only have you drawn the design for your future, but you are also the one who will bring it to life. So the time to act is now. The longer you wait, the harder it will be to accomplish. When you start this construction your focus has to be on one thing and one thing only, refuse to allow this edifice to ever fall again. This time you have to do whatever it takes. No matter what, you can't lose. Three things need to be present: You need a burning hot "I Will Until" attitude, the ability to pull that other person out of you, and to start immediately.

I Will Until

We've come to the end of this journey as we look at this final principle. A lot has been mentioned that will make your relaunch unstoppable; however, none of it matters if you lack fuel. Have you ever prepared for a long trip? You pack your bags, take out money for the trip, check your itinerary, check all your fluids, and know that you're good to go. To the novice you're good to go, but to the experienced traveller, one thing is missing from your checklist—gas for the car. See, the excitement of this trip will have you buzzing around like a bumble bee, all over the place frantically. If you're not careful, you'll go full throttle with little fuel in your tank. What do you mean, Rodney? The fuel that you need is the I Will Until. This is the drive that you need to push through, no matter what.

Many times we have watched movies where the car runs out of gas at the most inconvenient time. They took a detour that stretched the journey, or they failed to check before they left; something caused the fuel to be spent. Now they are stuck and have to leave their car to go find gas. Many of us have been there.

We started this journey with excellent intentions, but intentions won't fuel you all the way. Intentions are the motive that start the journey, but in this season, they have to be paired with a laser focus. One of the best ways to explain this is to consider a barber. The average barber will give you a good haircut, and give you a clean line up, just using the trimmer. A distinguished barber will take his time to make the cut perfect, use the trimmers, but add the last element—the razor. This is to further define the already sharp line up. The distinguished barber knows that you are a walking commercial, and if you leave his chair, you have to look like a million bucks. To you it may just be a cut, to him it's how he eats. His family is counting on him to make it through. So his I Will Until is to support his family. He can't give you an average haircut because his family isn't average.

In the movie *The Pursuit of Happiness,* John Gardener was evicted, slept in subway bathrooms with his son, got hit by a car, his wife left, he gets arrested for a parking ticket violation and has to spend the night in jail, goes to an interview not properly dressed and covered in paint, but he knew I Will Until. He knew that no matter what he had to win; his son was counting on him. He couldn't afford to be off, he couldn't afford to quit. Gardner realized that life had more to offer and he would not stop until he achieved it.

Many of us have thrown in the towel because we didn't have this type of drive. Many are halfway there and want to go back or even quit. Why? You're halfway to your destiny. The same energy it will take you to go back is the same energy you can use to finish. It's hard! *And?* This misconception that it's too hard, so I'll quit, has to be thrown out the window. You were given this dream for a reason, work at it until you win. The difference between those who win and those who don't is the choice made that *losing is not an option.* A mother will never quit on her child because she remembers the labor, she remembers the pain, she remembers the process. You are too far in your process to have an abortion.

Will it hurt? Yes. Will you cry? Yes. Will you sweat? Yes. However, when you birth this new you it will all be worth it.

Have you ever heard women share their birthing stories? Have you ever seen the pride that they have when they see the results of their labor? Inside them was the makings of a doctor, lawyer, president, business owner. If we look at the greats:

Michael Jordan, Tom Brady, Oprah Winfrey, Bill Gates, Mark Zuckerberg, and the like, what if their moms had quit too early? You have no idea what's in you, so commit to the process until you see manifestation.

Commit

I was asked several years ago, "Are you committed?" I answered yes. They asked the same question again, and I answered yes again. They asked a third time, and again I answered yes. How committed are you? To me, all commitment was the same. Until they explained the question. They said two types of commitment exist, and their example was the traditional breakfast sandwich. You normally have eggs, cheese, meat and bread. The bread went through the following process: mixing the dough, proofing, and baking, a pretty basic process. The eggs came from a chicken, another simple process. Cheese is a dairy product coming from the milk of a cow, add preservatives, and process, again a fairly simple process. However, the meat is something different. That bacon, sausage, and scrapple were all animals that had to die in order to extract the meat of the breakfast.

Once it was explained that way it all made sense. I had to ask myself was I *totally committed or partially involved?* Little effort or involvement was needed for the bread, eggs and cheese; however, the cow-chicken-pig-turkey had to die…an all-in commitment. Are you all in? Have you decided that this time you're "In it to Win it?" Too many times we live life with a noncommittal attitude, willing to do the least amount of work possible but expecting greatness. Long gone are the days when you can be partially committed and yield great results. Your microwave, instant-gratification days are over. It's time to roll up your sleeves, tighten up your belt, pull up your bootstraps and get to work. You've cried too many tears to play small. Get ready. It's Game Time!

Start Now

All of this information you have read up to this point is valuable. You have been given a number of principles and theories that will transform you from your rock bottom broken state, to realizing the new you. Like a coach's playbook, all these principles and theories are just markings on paper. They mean absolutely nothing until they are matched with corresponding actions to bring them to life. They are the routines to be practiced repeatedly until they become instinctual responses. They become the new foundation on which you build the rest of your life. None of this matters: the time you spent reading, the notes you've taken, the tears you've cried—if you're not going to get up and start now.

I've heard the phrase "knowledge is power." While it may have some validity, that same knowledge is useless if never applied. Libraries are all full of books that give you knowledge. The interesting thing is that many have gone to school and received different degrees and certifications. They've spent a great deal of time and energy reading, writing papers, taking tests. They do whatever it takes to pass and graduate, but what is it all worth if it is never being used.

Pull That Other Person

I've heard the term "Beast Mode" over and over again when it comes to grinding to win. It is pushing past what you see as your limits. It is ignoring the short term pain for long term gain. The pain you have felt up to this point is nothing compared to what you're about to feel. You're digging deeper than you ever have before. You're moving past the pain, failures, shortcomings, obstacles and hurdles. This is where it all matters, this is where you have to pull that other person out of you. This is the version of you that fights regardless of the brick wall that you're facing.

See, no matter how hard you have worked, someone was buried deep inside you that needs to come out. It's that person who pushes their commitment, dedication, and ambition to another level. It's that fight to make average nonexistent in the atmosphere around them. Mediocrity and average have stolen your destiny from you, and you now have a chance to get it back. You can't approach this fight all delicate and weak; you have to possess that animalistic beast passion. This is about to be a dog fight to the finish; the interesting part is that the fight will prove who wanted it more—your fears or you. Sharp shooters, assassins, and marksmen have one thing in common, when they lock on and they have their target in sight, it's over. I dare you to look in the mirror and get mad, get frustrated with average, get annoyed with mediocrity, get the beast and fight back. Get that Incredible Hulk out of you; we all have that switch. Why have you been so afraid to flip the switch? Your time is now… It's Beast Mode Time!

<u>What Other Choice Do You Have?</u>

You've tried every option and none of them have worked for you up to this point. You've negotiated and compromised everything, and it's gotten you on the ground looking up. So what about gambling on yourself? What about taking a calculated risk to make this time what it needs to be—your chance to show up and win. You've been beaten in every round before this one. They have counted you a loss, but you know better.

In the movie *Southpaw*, Billy Hope loses everything, literally everything. His wife dies, his daughter is taken away from him, his belongings are stripped from him, he is down to nothing. In his comeback he had to swallow his pride and face the man in the mirror. He ended up in a place where he had just fought a charity fight and was offered a title match, a chance to get back to where he was before. This time he was humbled by all he'd lost, so he was ready to jump in immediately. He had no time to waste, he had to act on it at that moment.

You're in the same position. Life has given you a second chance to make that comeback you have always wanted. You can choose to do one of two things: sit and wait for life to hand you an opportunity or get off your hind parts and act now. What I have come to understand is that life isn't obligated to repeat itself. So grab the bull by the horns and make this comeback one that your haters talk about for years to come. Start now!

Let's Recap:

Nothing that will cut into the future happens by accident. It is all because of an action or series of actions you perform now. If you're really looking for this to be your last time in this position, make a declaration to refuse to ever let this rock bottom define you. This is how:

1. Stand firm on the principle I Will Until. Nothing will stop you from here on, nothing will hold you back, not even yourself.

2. Commit to the process. Be all in, be willing to die for the cause of you. When it's all said and done, let your name be known as the one who gave it all you had and then some.

---

3. Start now. Tomorrow is never promised. Move like you don't have a tomorrow to look forward to. Put passion behind your drive and launch now. You've been beaten up to this point; it's time you fight back. Your time to swing back at the life, fears, failures, and shortcomings is *now*.

Conclusion

It's been an interesting journey. We have learned so much over the last seven chapters. If you have made it this far, you have come to realize that the only way to really make this mark different is to face the music. Everything spelled out in this book serves as a blueprint. This blueprint will be nothing but a series of words if never applied. Time to be the general contractor and make the blueprint come alive. Take the time to bet on yourself and win. The fight in you is far greater than your rock bottom, so it's time to put aside your ego and your shortcomings and show the world that your "setback was only temporary... I've made the necessary adjustments and alignments... it's time for my comeback."

Stand back. This rocket is getting ready to launch... course is set, destination is locked in, count down has started ...

5

4

3

2

1

See you on the better side of victory!

When You've Hit Rock Bottom, Smile You're Not Falling Anymore